NATIONAL GEOGRAPHIC

D0602855

I Work at Night

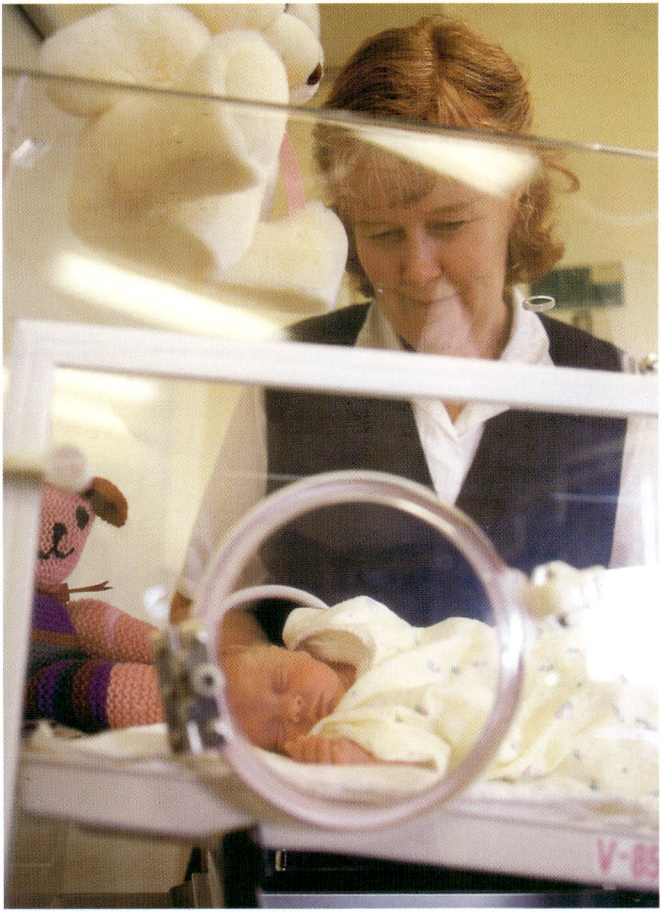

Leroy Taylor

I work at night.
I bake bread.

I work at night.
I clean offices.

I work at night.
I drive a truck.

I work at night.
I serve food.

street cleaner

I work at night.
I clean streets.

I work at night.
I help people.

Picture Index

baker 2

cleaning woman . . . 3

driver 4

nurse 7

server 5

street cleaner. 6